ROOM
LOVE

by Heather Wutschke

50 DIY Projects to Design Your Space

Capstone Young Readers
a capstone imprint

Table of Contents

INTRODUCTION

Fab Furniture & FABRICS

Storage & ORGANIZATION STATIONS

80

86

74

Dreamy DRESSING ZONE

Way Cool WALLS

Glam Decor & MORE

Welcome to
ROOM LOVE

Statistics say you will spend at least one third of your life in your bedroom — ONE THIRD! So why not make it the most amazing place you can imagine and fill it with things that make you happy? Your bedroom should reflect your personality. It should be a room where you can't wait to curl up with a good book, an inspiring space for you to get ready to face the world, and the place where your friends all want to hang out. Show your room a little love and it will become a place where you love to be!

This project guide is designed to help you develop your own personal style and make your room into a happier, cozier space that celebrates you. ROOM LOVE will help you achieve high style on any budget with upcycled, recycled, or made-from-scratch projects and crafts that you can do yourself. Each one is designed to help you develop and embrace your unique style. Happy DIY! And remember:

Everything in your room should bring you joy!

Create a MOOD BOARD

girl power

AWESOMENESS

Visualize your ideal room. Is it girly and pink? Soft and modern? Edgy and cool? Eclectic and full of different patterns? A great way to form a strong vision is to create a mood board.

Start gathering images and objects you are drawn to — patterns, color combinations, textures, furniture styles, clothing and jewelry, words that reflect your personality . . . anything that evokes emotion and screams YOU!

Supplies

photos, printed pictures, fabric scraps, scrapbook paper, paint swatches, quotes, etc.

scissors

canvas, board, or cardboard

glue or washi tape

Steps

1. Research: Look through photos, magazines, Pinterest, postcards, etc. Print or cut out images that inspire you. Include snips of scrap fabric, patterned paper, or paint swatches to capture color schemes you like.

2. Pull it all together: Position images on the board in an arrangement you like. Adhere each with glue or washi tape. Add textures, color swatches, notes, favorite words, and anything else that defines your style.

3. Place the mood board in your room to help inspire you as you make design decisions. This mood board can help you determine the overall look and feel of your new space.

START FRESH

Declutter and REARRANGE

Before you get creative, you've got to get decluttered! Most of us have more stuff than we know what to do with (and definitely more than we need). All that clutter adds stress to your life! Eliminating extra stuff from your room will clear the canvas and allow you to create a space that rejuvenates you instead of distracting you.

Tips

* Work your way around your room. Every area should get a thorough inspection. Don't forget the closet and under the bed!

* Check with a parent before throwing anything away. Ask about giving away items of value or putting them into storage if they're not working in your room.

* Set up three piles: one for KEEP, one for GIVE AWAY, and one for THROW AWAY. Throw out anything torn, stained, or broken. Sell or donate anything that someone else can use. Keep only the items that you love or really need. Say goodbye to anything you haven't used in a year.

* Consolidate and eliminate! Why do you have four jewelry boxes or five black sweaters that all look the same? Pick your favorites to keep and give the others away.

* Sort like things together: All your books should be in one area, all your art supplies in another spot, etc. Every shelf and drawer should have a purpose.

* Before putting away the things you're keeping, clean every surface. Clean as if your snoopiest relative were coming for a visit. Utilize those weird vacuum nozzle attachments that have never been used!

After you've decluttered, making efficient and creative use of your space will set you on the path to transforming your room into your happy place. Take a look around. Is your bed too close to a chilly window? Is there good lighting for your study area? Do you have places to store everything? Experiment with different layouts on paper before you start moving furniture around.

Supplies

tape measure

ruler

pencil (and eraser!)

paper

scissors

Steps

1. Measure your room. Draw the outline of your room on a piece of paper. (Eg., for an 8 x 10-foot room, draw a box 8 x 10 inches.) Don't forget the closet!

2. Mark doors, windows, outlets, etc., on the paper.

3. Measure your furniture. Cut smaller pieces of paper to represent furniture using the foot-to-inch ratio again. (If your bed is 6 x 4 feet, cut out a rectangle that is 6 x 4 inches.)

4. Get creative! Move furniture pieces around the paper until you find the best arrangement.

Tip

Want to try a digital layout? Check out these free apps: RoomSketcher, Floorplanner, Sweet Home 3D, Floor Plan Creator, and MagicPlan.

outlet

closet

door

window

outlet

Fab Furniture
& FABRICS

Add warmth and shine to your room with reinvented furniture and cozy fabrics. Create a sanctuary where you can feel calm, nurtured, and recharged.

Dresser MAKEOVER

This project is a great hand-me-down furniture solution! Take something outdated or boring and turn it into something beautiful and unique.

Supplies

dresser or any piece of furniture
  you want to stencil
drop cloth
medium-grade sandpaper
slightly damp paper towels
paint with primer for base color (satin finish)
paint tray
paintbrush
stencil
painter's tape
acrylic paint for stencil
stencil brush

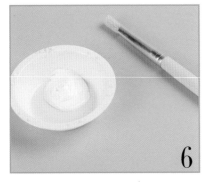

6

7

Tip

Don't overload your stencil brush with paint or it will seep under the stencil edges.

Steps

1. In a well-ventilated area, put furniture on drop cloth to protect the floor.

2. Sand furniture if you are going to paint it before stenciling.

3. After sanding, wipe the surface down with damp paper towels. Allow to dry.

4. Apply two coats of paint, letting it dry between coats. Let dry overnight before stenciling.

5. Plan out stencil design and position first stencil where you want it on furniture, adhering it with painter's tape so it doesn't shift.

6. Dip stencil brush in stencil paint and gently press down directly onto the stencil. Remove stencil and rinse and dry it while the paint is still wet.

7. Place stencil in the next place you want it and repeat process until you have the design you like.

Furry Kitty
⇒DESK CHAIR⇐

Give your desk chair some personality with this fun furniture makeover. Fabulous fur makes for a cozy place to sit and transforms a plain chair into a style statement!

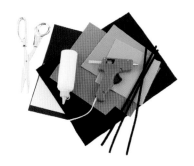

Supplies

chair (office-style chair works best)	green and black felt
2 yards white faux fur	pink craft foam
scissors	black pipe cleaners
hot glue gun and glue	cardboard

Steps

1. Measure and cut a piece of fur long and wide enough to cover the front and back of the chair back, folded over at the top.

2. Glue sides together to form a sort of pillow case. Glue bottom of pillow case once fitted onto chair back. From inside the folded fabric, pull top corners in to make them more rounded.

3. Repeat for the seat. You will need to cut a slit in the bottom to allow for the chair leg. Glue the slit together after going around the chair leg.

4. Cut eyes using the green and black felt. Layer eye pieces, then glue them together.

5. Cut foam to make mouth, nose, and inside of ears.

6. Cut pipe cleaners to create whiskers and mouth.

7. Cut two triangle ear shapes out of cardboard. Cut and glue fur to cover them. Then glue pink triangles to ears. Glue ears to the top of the chair.

8. Attach the face to the chair by sewing or gluing.

Patterned BOOKCASE

Give an inexpensive bookshelf a facelift with vibrant patterned paper framed with funky washi tape. It's easy to change up and redo whenever you feel like refreshing the color or design.

Supplies

bookshelf

slightly damp rag

tape measure

scrapbook paper

scissors

decoupage glue

brush for decoupage

plastic scraper or plastic card

Steps

1. Clean shelf with damp rag.

2. Measure the shelf openings. Cut scrapbook paper to fit the back wall of each shelf.

3. Put a layer of decoupage glue on the back wall of the first shelf. You don't need to go all the way to the edge as the glue will spread a little.

4. Immediately lay the first sheet of scrapbook paper onto the back of the shelf, making sure paper is straight. Using the scraper or plastic card, start in the center and scrape outward, pressing gently to remove air bubbles. Continue until the paper adheres to the back of the shelf.

5. Repeat this step on each shelf until fully covered. Allow to dry.

6. For a more permanent look, use decoupage glue over the top of each paper.

Gold-Accented
FURNITURE

Dip-dyed legs of tables or chairs can make a huge impact in your room. It's a super simple way to add sophistication to your space. Use gold, silver, or any color you want to create a personalized look. Turn old, hand-me-down furniture into something you love!

Supplies

chair or table

medium-grade sandpaper

slightly damp paper towels

drop cloth

spray paint

tape measure or ruler

pencil

painter's tape

gold acrylic paint

small paintbrush

Steps

If you're just adding gold tips, you can skip to step 4.

1. Put down drop cloth in well-ventilated area. Sand furniture.

2. Wipe down with damp paper towels. Allow to dry.

3. Paint table with 2–3 light coats of spray paint, allowing it to dry between coats. Let dry overnight.

4. Turn furniture upside down. Measure 5–10 inches from the end of each leg, depending on how much accent you want. Mark with a pencil. Apply painter's tape around legs below pencil line for a clean edge.

5. Apply three coats of gold acrylic paint with paintbrush.

6. Allow paint to dry and then remove painter's tape.

Tip

Replace an old knob with a new one from a hardware store. They come in endless varieties!

Washi Tape
MAKEOVER

Use this colorful adhesive to revamp just about any item in your room. It's quick and cheap — and easy to change up if next week you decide you're mad for polka dots instead of stripes! If you want the surface to become more permanent, you can add a decoupage sealer.

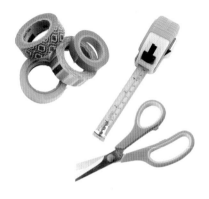

Supplies

furniture

slightly damp paper towel

washi tape

scissors

tape measure or ruler

pencil

Steps

1. Wipe surface with paper towel and let dry.

2. Plan your design. Create a pattern or just do a washi trim around the edges.

3. Tape away! Use a ruler or tape measure if you are worried about crooked lines. Measure and lightly mark with a pencil on each end of the table to guide the washi tape.

BEFORE

1

3

22

Dreamy BEDDING

Your bedding is essential in providing a good night's sleep — the cozier, the better! Make your bed look like a magazine spread with lots of pillows and create your perfect Cloud Nine.

1. Bedspread
Choose a bedspread or comforter in a color you love because the bed is the centerpiece of a bedroom.

2. Pillows
Find a sleeping pillow that supports your neck and leaves you feeling refreshed.

3. Throw Pillows
Layer several throw pillows on your bed to create a cozy nest effect.

4. Mix and Match
Combine colors, patterns, and textures to add variety.

5. Blanket
Keep a snuggly blanket nearby for chilly nights or rainy afternoons reading in bed.

6. Make the Bed!
Make your bed every morning so you're not tempted to hop back in!

Hand-Painted Ombre
PILLOW

Throw pillows can be pricey, but not if you make your own! Take a plain pillow and give it a designer look with a sophisticated gradient paint scheme.

Supplies

drop cloth

ruler

pencil

white throw pillow or white
  pillow case if using bed pillow

paint sponge

3–4 shades of the same
  color acrylic paint

3

Tip

If you don't have 3 shades of same color paint, make your own by adding amounts of white to the main color to get different shades.

4

Steps

1. Prepare painting area by laying out drop cloth to work on.

2. Using a ruler and lightly drawing with a pencil, divide the pillow into 3–4 vertical sections (depending on the number of colors you have).

3. Starting at one end, sponge paint a vertical stripe of darkest color onto pillow.

4. Sponge paint second-darkest color next to the first.

5. Blend edges of colors together with sponge. Repeat with remaining colors. Continue blending the colors and let paint dry overnight.

6. Add the pillow to the arrangement on your bed!

5

Boho BED SKIRT

Add a bit of stylish whimsy to your bed to dress it up! These tassels will give your bedding a trendy new look — and might even inspire you to make your bed each morning to show off your bed skirt bling!

Supplies

yarn in 1–3 colors that coordinate
    with bedding
7 x 3-inch piece of cardboard
ruler
scissors
beaded string or ribbon for accent

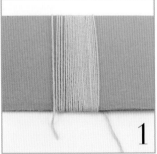

Steps

1. Leaving a 2-inch tail hanging down, hold yarn in place with your thumb as you wrap the yarn up and over the cardboard. Wrap around 15–20 times, with the yarn ending at the bottom.

2. Cut two 14-inch pieces of the beaded string or ribbon. Lay it over the wrapped yarn loop.

3. Cut a 5-inch piece of yarn and slide it under the top of the wrapped yarn loop and string/ribbon. Tie it around all in a double knot to form the top of the tassel.

4. Cut the bottom loops to create the tassels. Remove the cardboard.

5. Trim any shaggy ends and repeat to start a new tassel. Depending on how far apart you want the tassels, 25–35 will be enough for a twin bed.

6. Tie a long piece of yarn all the way around the perimeter of the mattress. Attach each tassel to that yarn by taking one strand from each side of the tassel knot and tying it around to the yarn perimeter, spacing evenly.

DIY CANOPY

Give your bed the princess treatment with this easy DIY canopy.
You can repurpose old sheer curtains found at secondhand stores.

Supplies

sheer curtains

curtain rod (any length will work)

brackets for curtain rod

hammer

nails

ribbon

tacks

Tip

Take wrinkles out of brand new fabric by hanging in the bathroom during a hot shower!

Steps

1. Thread curtains onto a curtain rod. Make sure any seams in the curtains are facing the wall.

2. Have someone hold the curtain rod above the bed where you want it. Mark lightly on the wall with a pencil where the brackets should go. Make sure it's straight across and not slanted.

3. With a parent's permission, use hammer to nail the brackets to the wall. Put the curtain rod on the brackets.

4. Pull curtains at least partway closed at the top to create a triangular draping above the bed.

5. Affix the curtains to the headboard to keep them open, or make your own curtain "tiebacks" by tying each side with a ribbon. You can tack the back of the ribbon to the wall behind it to keep the curtains open.

Tip

Old dresses or shirts with pretty fabric that no longer fit can be cut into strips and added to your curtains!

Stylish
CURTAINS

Give your windows a one-of-a-kind refresh using all your favorite colors and fabrics! Mix and match materials until you find the perfect combination to capture your style. The curtain could also work in place of a closet door.

Supplies

tape measure

scissors

ribbon, lace, and fabrics from
old sheets, scarves, etc.

Steps

1. Measure the distance from the curtain rod to the floor.

2. Cut strips of fabric, ribbon, and lace to the length needed to reach the floor. Tie multiple strips together if needed for length. (You can also tie knots to shorten some strips and add texture.) Vary the widths of the pieces for a fun mixture.

3. Take down the curtain rod and begin tying fabric, ribbon, and lace in knots onto the rod. Make sure to vary the colors of the fabric as you tie them on.

4. Once curtain rod is full, hang back up and enjoy your funky new curtain.

Storage &
ORGANIZATION
STATIONS

Getting creative with storage
in your room can help you
organize your space and
maximize its functionality.

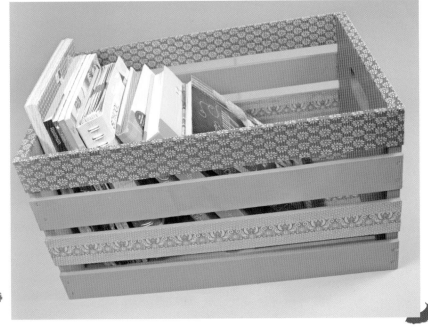

Succulent
BOOKENDS

Books falling off shelves? Secure them in style with these gorgeous faux plant bookends. No watering required! You can change out the colored glass beads with pretty rocks or vintage marbles to refresh the look.

1

Supplies

clear glass container (or small canning jar)

marbles, rocks, or colored glass beads

fake succulent plants

2

Steps

1. Clean glass container.

2. Add colored glass, rocks, or marbles to container to make it heavy enough to hold up books.

3. Cut the stems of the succulents a few inches below the plant so that you can stick them into the marbles to anchor them.

4. Display your favorite books with your new bookends!

3

Sunglasses HOLDER

No one likes a pair of scratched sunglasses, right? Here's a great way to store and show off your fabulous shades. Quick and easy — and it makes artwork out of your eyewear!

Supplies

11 x 14-inch picture frame
ice pick or thumbtack
4 screw eyes
wire

Steps

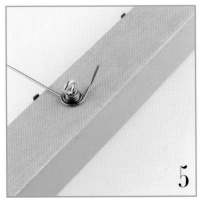

1. Remove backing and glass from frame. Be very careful when removing glass as edges will be sharp.

2. Lay frame flat on floor. Arrange sunglasses in frame to determine where you would like the two rows to be.

3. Flip the frame over. Use the ice pick or thumbtack to create holes on each side where you want the wires to attach.

4. Insert a screw eye into each hole.

5. Wrap wire through and around one screw a few times to secure. Pull wire tight to the other side of the frame. Wrap wire onto the opposite screw. Repeat for second row.

6. Set frame in the window or ask if you can nail it to your wall.

Drawer
DIVIDERS

Have all your drawers become junk drawers because you throw whatever you find into them? Put old boxes to work and give every drawer order and purpose with these cost-nothing, style-boosting dividers. Use different-size boxes depending on what goes in each drawer — smaller boxes for craft supplies or hair supplies, larger boxes for socks and underwear.

Supplies

tape measure or ruler
cereal or other boxes
scissors
contact paper

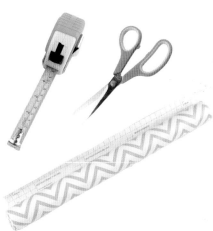

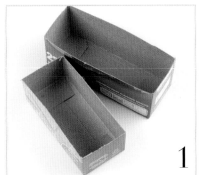

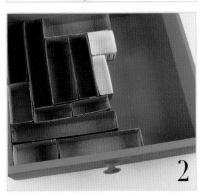

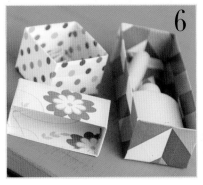

Steps

1. Cut the top and bottom off of each box to get two dividers from each. Cut them short enough to fit inside the drawer and allow it to close easily.

2. Arrange boxes in drawer to see how they fit best.

3. Put a sheet of contact paper pattern-side down on workspace. (Do not remove the backing yet.) Set first box on the contact paper.

4. Cut the paper so it will wrap over the sides to cover the inner and outer sides of the box.

5. Now remove backing from contact paper. Fold up the sides and stick the paper to the box.

6. Measure inside bottom of box. Cut contact paper to fit. Remove backing and stick to inside bottom of box.

7. Repeat until each box is covered. Place boxes in the drawer and organize your things!

Tip

You can store things in the oatmeal container. This will also help to weigh it down so it won't tip over easily.

Hair Accessory
HOLDER

Headbands are easy to wear, stylish, and can save you if you only have a second to do your hair before you rush off to school. This funky display shows off your headwear and keeps it handy so you can grab, style, and go!

Supplies

pillar candle holder

acrylic paint

small paintbrush

2 12 x 12-inch sheets of
  scrapbook paper

scissors

tape measure

empty 42 oz. oatmeal
  container (large size)

decoupage glue

brush for decoupage

plastic scraper or plastic card

hot glue gun and glue

○ ○

Steps

1. Paint pillar and allow to dry.

2. Cut both sheets of paper so they're the height of the container (9 ½ inches). Leave length as is — sheets will overlap.

3. Spread decoupage on sides of container. Line up the short side of one sheet of paper with the height of container. Wrap it around and smooth out with scraper. Put on second sheet of paper to cover rest of container. You'll need to apply another layer of decoupage where the sheets overlap. Smooth with scraper.

4. Spread more decoupage over the top of both sheets of paper. Allow to dry.

5. Use hot glue gun to adhere oatmeal container to the pillar. Put on the lid.

6. Put headbands around container and fill the container with hair supplies!

Tip

Make sure the fabric is porous enough for earrings to hook and remove without snagging.

Easy Peasy
EARRING HOLDER

If all your earrings are jumbled together in a box, separated from their partners, reunite them and show them off with this clever DIY display. Add it to a photo collage with other frames on your wall and it becomes a work of art!

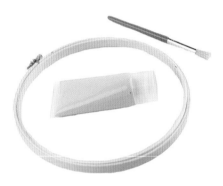

Supplies

embroidery hoop

acrylic paint

paintbrush

fabric (thin works best)

scissors

Steps

1. Remove screw from the top of the embroidery hoop so the two wood pieces come apart. Paint each piece and let dry.

2. Place the smaller hoop on a flat surface.

3. Lay the fabric pattern-side up over this hoop.

4. Place the larger hoop over the fabric. Press down so the small hoop comes up through the large hoop and fits together.

5. Replace screw and tighten. This will hold the fabric in place.

6. Trim excess fabric from the back of the hoop.

7. Poke your earrings through the fabric. For earrings with backs, you can place those on the earring posts from the back side of the fabric.

Driftwood
JEWELRY HANGER

Don't hide your jewelry in a box — make it into DIY wall art! Display your favorite pieces and show your artistic skill by painting a piece of driftwood in coordinating colors and patterns.

Supplies

large piece of driftwood

acrylic paint

paintbrush

painter's tape

4–6 craft hooks

string or ribbon

scissors

nail or tack

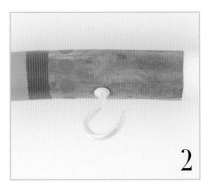

Steps

1. Pick a color palette and paint a design on the driftwood. Use painter's tape to paint clean stripes. Allow to dry.

2. Gently press hooks into bottom of the stick, screwing them in. Make sure hooks are pointing forward when done.

3. Cut string or ribbon and tie to each end.

4. Display favorites necklaces or bracelets on the hooks. Ask a parent if you can nail it on your wall, or hang it from a tackboard.

Hanging STORAGE

Instead of scattering things all over your dresser top, load up these fun buckets with odds and ends and keep your surfaces clear. Pick pretty colored fabric to give the buckets some style. Consider hand-lettered labels to assign each bucket a task.

Supplies

3 small metal buckets

large piece of paper (for template)

pencil (or white crayon for dark fabric)

scissors

fabric

drop cloth

spray adhesive

yarn or shoelaces

Steps

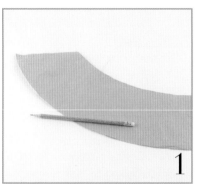

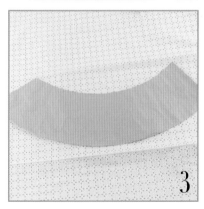

1. To make a template, lay one bucket on its side on the paper. Line up the metal seam of the bucket with the edge of the paper. Trace the path it makes as you roll the bucket along the paper. Stop when you've reached the seam again. Cut this shape out.

2. Wrap the cut paper around the bucket to make sure it fits. Trim off any excess. This is the template.

3. Trace template onto the backside of the fabric. (If the fabric has a direction to it, make sure the top of the template is toward the "up" side.) Cut the traced shape out of the fabric. Cut two more just like it.

4. In a well-ventilated area, lay the drop cloth on a flat surface. Lay fabric pattern-side down. Lay the bucket on its side on the fabric.

5. Spray adhesive onto the entire piece of fabric and line short side up with the bucket seam. Press down and begin rolling the bucket along the fabric, smoothing it out as you go.

6. Hang buckets from yarn or a shoelace and tie to hooks or curtain rod.

Magnetic
⇒ MAKEUP BOARD ⇐

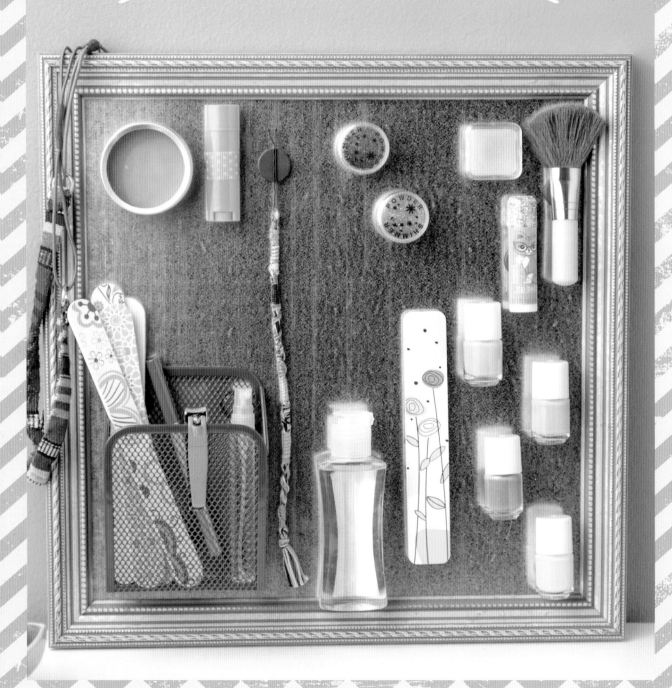

Declutter your drawers and dresser tops and create easy access to lip balms, lotions, deodorant, and other things you use every day by magnetizing them! Frame all your essentials for a fun and clever boutique display.

Supplies

12 x 12-inch picture frame
butter knife
12 x 12-inch sheet metal
hot glue gun and glue
small magnets

Steps

1. If the frame has tabs on the back, use butter knife to lift them and carefully remove the glass. Glass edges will be sharp.

2. Replace glass with sheet metal and resecure back of frame.

3. Find makeup or other items you want to keep handy.

4. Glue a magnet onto back of each item.

5. Organize items onto sheet metal. Your morning routine will be a snap!

Treasures

Treasure
BOX

Everyone needs a special place to store and honor personal keepsakes. A beautiful, handmade box is even more special. Place family heirlooms, birthday cards, unique coins, or any special objects inside to keep them safe.

Supplies

large shoe box
patterned paper
   (enough to cover
   entire box)
pencil
ruler
scissors
newspapers

decoupage glue
brush for decoupage
plastic scraper or plastic card
envelope
embellishments such as
   stickers, gold pen, washi
   tape, glitter, etc.

Steps

1. Trace bottom of box on the backside of the patterned paper. Cut out.
2. Measure and cut pieces to fit the rest of the box, including lid. For the sides, make pieces long enough to cover both inside and outside. Paper will fold over top edges.
3. Lay out newspapers to protect work surface.
4. Starting with the bottom of the box, use brush to spread glue on the box surface and press patterned paper onto it. Smooth out any wrinkles with scraper.
5. Repeat with each side of box. For sides, crease the tops to make sharp edges of folded paper, then glue down.
6. Glue envelope to inside of lid. (Use it to store special notes or letters!) Add any embellishments.
7. Put your treasures inside the box!

Pretty
CHARGING STATION

Phones, devices, and all the cords that go with them can really clutter up surfaces. Get organized with this charging station that hides annoying cords and keeps your technology tidy!

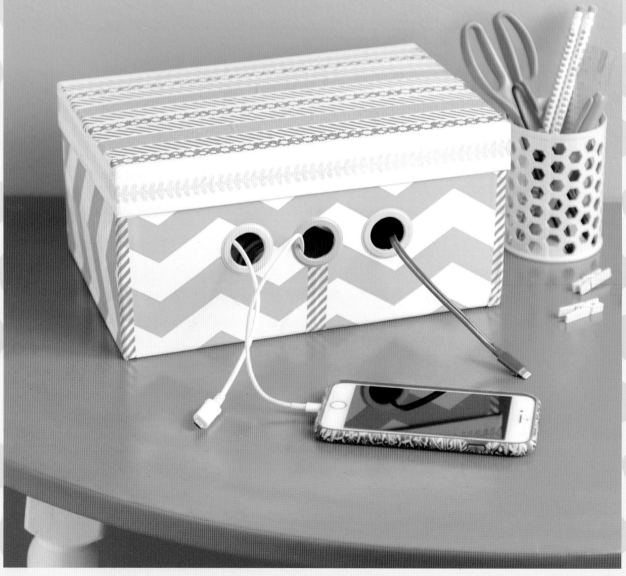

Supplies

Safety First
Make sure power strip and chargers do not produce heat. Ask a parent whether they're safe inside a box.

decorated shoe box
4 1-inch metal grommets
pencil
utility knife
hot glue gun and glue
power strip

Steps

1. Turn box so that its side faces up. Place three grommets where you would like them on the box. Trace the inner circle of each with a pencil. Flip the box over and trace one grommet on the opposite side for the power strip cord to go out the back.

2. Ask a parent to help you cut out the holes with the utility knife.

3. Use a glue gun to place the grommets in the holes.

4. Put a power strip into the box and push the end of the cord through the hole in back.

5. Collect all your chargers and place them into the box with the cords coming out through the front grommets for the devices.

*Safety notes: *Plug chargers in only for the time it takes to charge *Don't connect too many chargers at one time *Disconnect the extension cord from the outlet when not in use to avoid overheating the box*

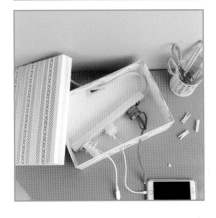

Tip

Use individually, stack, or hang. You can also add labels to the crates to help organize like items.

Wooden Crate
STORAGE

You can find affordable wooden crates just about anywhere. Paint the inside, decoupage the outside, add stencils . . . the options are endless. This super versatile project is a fun way to express your creativity with functional results!

Supplies

wooden crates

medium-grade sandpaper

slightly damp paper towels

drop cloth

acrylic paints

paintbrushes

variety of washi tapes

scissors

Steps

1. Sand each wood crate so that the wood is smooth.

2. Wipe down crates with damp paper towels. Allow to dry.

3. On the drop cloth, paint the crates. Use two layers for good coverage, allowing paint to dry thoroughly between coats.

4. Select a variety of patterned washi tapes and apply to slats, creating your own pattern. You might want to skip every other slat, or only use tape around the top and bottom edges.

5. Put your belongings in your fun new crates!

Dreamy
DRESSING
ZONE

A mirror, good lighting, and easy access to your clothes make for quick transformations from bedhead to beautiful!

Personalized DRESSING AREA

Want to feel famous? Create a movie-star worthy dressing room with a mirror, flattering lighting, and all your favorite accessories at your fingertips. Your personalized dressing area will help you get stage-ready in no time!

1. Good lighting

Good light is essential in a dressing area. Choose a spot near a window or an overhead light to make sure you're not wearing one black sock and one navy sock.

2. Mirror

A full-length mirror makes it easiest to see your whole ensemble at once and help you decide whether to go with the funky boots or the comfy sneakers.

3. Rug

A cozy rug will keep your toes warm on chilly mornings and add a splash of style and comfort to your dressing space.

4. Hooks

Keep belts, purses, and other accessories handy with hooks. You can also hang tomorrow's outfit there so it's ready to slip into when you roll out of bed.

5. Shelf Storage

A nearby shelf is a great spot to store extra items like hats, jewelry, and inspirational images to keep you looking your best!

6. Clock

To help you keep track of time, keep a clock in sight and stay on schedule!

Washi Tape
HANGERS

Add some style and organization to your closet with these pretty hangers. Shower curtain hooks are a cheap, space-saving solution to consolidate hats and tank tops onto one hanger.

Supplies

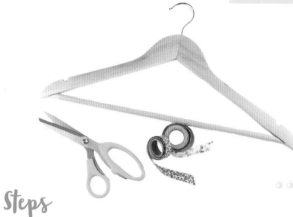

wooden hangers

fabric washi tape

scissors

shower curtain rings

Steps

1. Start near the hook and wrap washi tape around the wooden part of the hanger, working toward the end. You can wrap straight from the roll or cut tape into strips and wrap one at a time. Continue wrapping until you have covered the entire wooden portion.

2. For organizing tank tops and hats, hang shower curtain rings on the bottom of the hanger and hook items to the rings. For scarves, simply tie them onto the hanger.

Yarn Bomb HANGERS

Upcycle flimsy wire hangers into something beautiful and nonslip for those tops that never stay put. Using variegated yarn is a simple way to incorporate many colors.

Tip

To make the hanger thicker, stack 2–3 hangers together before wrapping with yarn.

Supplies

wire hangers
yarn
scissors
hot glue gun and glue

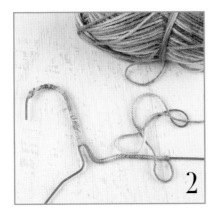

Steps

1. Tie yarn to the neck of the hanger

2. Tightly wrap yarn around the hanger. As you wrap, use a dab of glue every now and then to keep yarn in place.

3. Wrap the yarn tightly to cover the entire hanger. Once fully covered, snip the end and glue to secure in place.

Outfit
PLANNER

Instead of rolling out of bed each morning and staring at your closet when you're half asleep, choose your outfits in advance. On weekends, look at your week ahead and decide what to wear each day. Monday mornings will be a breeze!

Supplies

Polaroid or any camera
   and printer
step stool
newspapers
12 x 9-inch canvas
acrylic paint (variety of colors)
large paintbrush
5 clothespins

small paintbrush
cardboard
scissors
tape
washi tape
gold pen
hot glue gun and glue

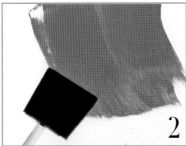

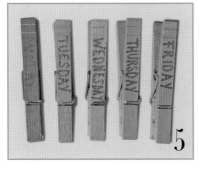

Steps

1. Take pictures of your favorite outfits, arranging your tops, bottoms, shoes, and accessories. Use the floor or a light-colored surface as a backdrop. Shoot pictures from overhead, standing on a stool if you need extra height. Print photos.

2. Put newspapers down on your work surface. Paint your canvas using large brush. Allow to dry.

3. Paint your clothespins using small brush. Allow to dry.

4. Use cardboard, scissors, and tape to make 2 small boxes to hold your photos. Make boxes short enough to allow tops of photos to show. Cover your boxes with washi tape.

5. Use gold pen to label your clothespins for each weekday, Monday through Friday.

6. Position boxes and clothespins on canvas with sample photos in place to determine how to space them. Then glue both boxes to the top of your canvas and each clothespin to the bottom of your canvas.

7. Use gold pen to make labels to categorize boxes for seasons or weather.

8. Plan your outfits for the following week by placing one on each clothespin. Add remaining photos to your boxes.

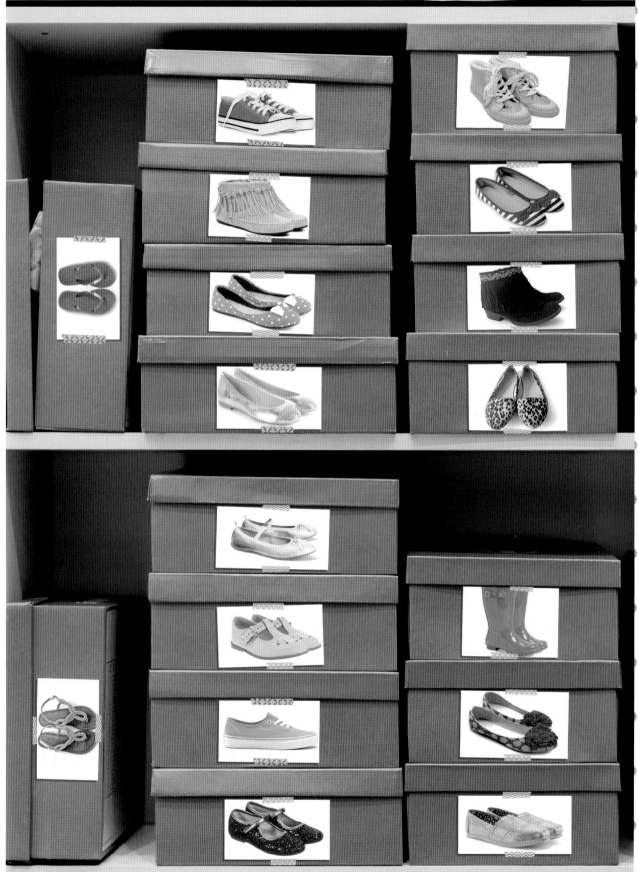

64

Boutique Shoe
ORGANIZING

No more digging for your left ballet flat in a messy shoe pile! Here is a simple, upcycled way to organize your shoe collection and keep stock of what you have. Add a cute bench nearby so you can sit and slip on your Cinderella slippers before dashing out the door.

Supplies

newspapers

shoe boxes

spray paint

camera and printer

washi tape

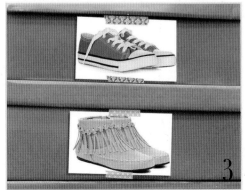

Steps

1. In a well-ventilated area, prepare work area by laying out newspapers. Spray paint each shoe box and lid. Allow to dry.

2. Snap a photo of each pair of shoes. Print photos.

3. Place shoes in boxes and attach matching photo to the end of each box with washi tape.

4. Stack boxes neatly or place on a shelf for easy access!

Way Cool
WALLS

Fill your walls with fun photos, special items, and unexpected surprises that show your fun side!

Rose
WALL CLOCK

Foam paper flowers are a simple, no-fuss way to add a pretty accent to a plain-Jane wall clock. In just minutes you can create dozens of DIY flowers to cover the frame of your clock.

Supplies

scissors

ruler

8 foam paper 9 x 6-inch sheets

    (1 sheet = 2 flowers)

hot glue gun and glue

wall clock

Steps

1. Measure and cut foam sheets into 4 x 4-inch squares. (A 9-inch clock will need about 16 squares, which will make 16 roses.)

2. Cut each square into a scalloped spiral.

3. Starting from the outside, roll the sheet of foam inward to construct a rose. Put a dab of glue at the end of the roll to hold the rose in its shape.

4. Once you have assembled enough roses to cover the frame of the clock, begin applying a dab of hot glue to the bottom of each rose. Stick each onto clock and repeat until the frame is full.

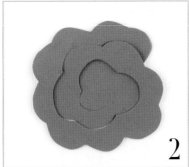

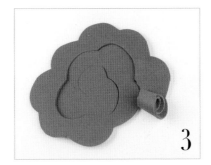

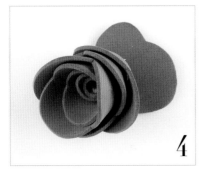

BE BRAVE

THANK YOU very MUCH

SOMETIMES YOU WIN SOMETIMES YOU LEARN

Happily ever After

GOOD VIBES ONLY

Carpe Diem

LIFE IS TOUGH BUT SO ARE YOU

DON'T FORGET TO BE AWESOME.

Wake up —AND— be awesome

THE REST OF MY LIFE THE BEST OF MY LIFE

XOXO

chin up smile on

STOP WISHING. START DOING.

Laugh

Hustle Baby

GO AFTER WHAT YOU WANT OR YOU WILL NEVER HAVE IT.

follow your dreams

enjoy the LITTLE things IN LIFE

YOU ARE very pretty TODAY

Do not compare yourself to others

HAPPY

V·I·N·T·A·G·E

girl power

Only you can make you HAPPY

GO AFTER WHAT YOU WANT OR YOU WILL NEVER HAVE IT.

CHILL it's only chaos

hel

MILE! you are ... red

Quote
WALL

Cover your wall with inspiration! Use it as a giant canvas to display favorite words, quotes, sayings, or symbols. Surround yourself with the positive energy of positive thoughts!

Oh yeah!
Let it go
choose joy
COURAGE
Dear
Make TODAY amazing

Supplies

computer and printer

printer paper

washi tape or glue dots

Steps

1. Make a list of your favorite quotes and sayings that you'd like to use.

2. Use a computer and type each quote so that it fills an 8 ½ x 11 sheet of paper. Play with different fonts and backgrounds to make each quote unique. Print.

3. Use washi tape or glue dots to stick each paper up to create a wall full of motivational messages!

Scrapbook
ACCENT WALL

Patterned paper is a great way to give a wall a new look without paint. Choose papers with colors that make you happy, and your accent wall will bring cheer to your room!

Supplies

slightly damp paper towels

step stool

tape measure

pencil

large assortment of 12 x 12-inch patterned
   scrapbook paper

glue dots (or clear tape)

Steps

1. Using damp paper towels, wipe down the wall you will be hanging the paper on. Use a step stool if you'd like the accent wall to go higher than you can reach.

2. Measure wall to determine how many scrapbook squares you will need. (If you have 3 square feet to work with, you'll need 9 sheets of paper.) Mark the corners of the area with pencil.

3. Lay out scrapbook paper on the floor to determine the best arrangement.

4. Place the glue dots (or a small piece of clear tape) on each paper and stick it on the wall in the order of your arrangement. Start with one column horizontally to get the position straight.

5. Continue until you have filled your wall with color!

Floral
MONOGRAM

A monogram is a great way to personalize your room — and doing it with a floral flair will give your room a fresh springtime feel year-round!

Supplies

newspapers

papier mâché letter
   for your name

empty egg crate or box
   (to prop up letter)

acrylic paint

paintbrush

utility knife

craft foam

hot glue gun and glue

artificial flowers

wire cutter

ribbon or yarn

scissors

nail or hook to hang

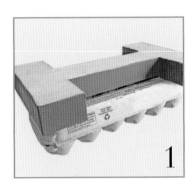

1

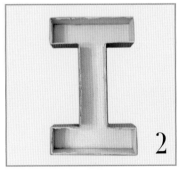

2

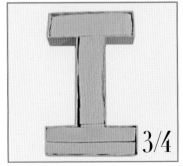

3/4

Steps

1. Prepare work area by laying out newspaper. Prop up papier mâché letter on egg crate and paint the sides. Do not paint the top surface of letter. Allow to dry.

2. As a parent's permission to use the utility knife to carefully cut out the top of the letter.

3. Cut pieces of foam to fill the inside of the letter. This can be done in sections.

4. Using glue gun, glue the foam sections into the letter.

5. With wire cutter, trim flower stems leaving just enough stem to stick into foam. Use different shapes, colors, and sizes. Hot glue any flowers that seem loose.

6. Hot glue a loop of ribbon to the back of the papier mâché letter and hang it on a nail or hook on your wall.

Confetti
WALL

Add pops of color to your wall for a bright, cheery, trendy look. Easy to make and easy to affix, you can play with the colors and arrangement until you achieve the look you want — whether it's bubbles in the breeze or balloons let loose!

Supplies

colored scrapbook paper
2 ½–4-inch circle shape to trace
  (or circle punch)
pencil
scissors
removable adhesive putty

Steps

1. Punch or trace and cut circles out of paper.

2. Place a small amount of putty on the back of each circle.

3. Stick the circles to the wall. Rearrange until you get just the right look!

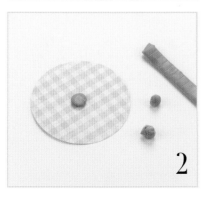

Framed
MANTRA

Is there a word or phrase that inspires you and brings you joy? Make your mantra into a one-of-a-kind work of art by painting, embellishing, and framing it!

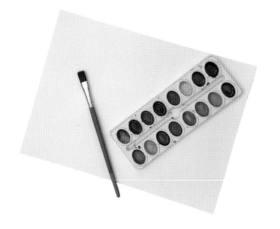

Supplies

watercolor paper cut to size
   of the frame
pencil
round sponge to create polka dots
watercolor or acrylic paints
paintbrushes
frame

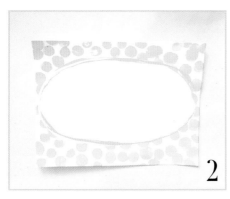

Steps

1. On paper, lightly sketch your word or phrase in pencil and draw an oval shape around it.

2. Use round sponge dipped in paint to create a polka dot pattern outside the oval.

3. Paint an oval stroke in a coordinating color.

4. Paint your message in a bold color. You can use a matching marker to touch up any areas you want to be more defined once the paint is dry.

5. Allow painting to dry, then frame and display it!

Fabric
BANNER

Drape your walls with color! Decorate a mirror, window, or dresser with a fun fabric banner to add style and warmth to your room.

Supplies

scissors
ruler
fabric scraps
string or twine
thumbtacks

Steps

1. Cut or rip strips of fabric in 10–12-inch lengths. Vary the widths from 1–3 inches.

2. Cut string or twine to the length you'd like your banner to be. If you'd like, tie each end to something to hold the string taut while you tie fabric on.

3. Begin tying fabric strips in knots onto the twine, leaving the ends dangling off both sides.

4. When finished, tie banner to your headboard posts or use thumbtacks to hang it on your wall.

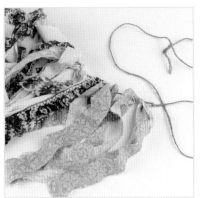

Gallery
WALL

the best
is yet
to come!
♥♥♥

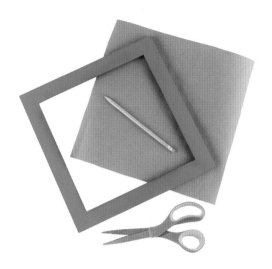

The right arrangement of art and photos can bring all your favorite pieces together into one cohesive display. Choose coordinating colors for your frames to tie it all together.

Supplies

favorite art pieces in colorful frames	scissors
craft paper	tape
pencil	hammer
	nails

Steps

1. Lay out framed art on the floor. Start with the boldest piece in the center and add other pieces around it.

2. Trace each frame onto a piece of craft paper, trim the paper to size, and tape to the wall in the planned arrangement. Make sure it fills the space nicely.

3. Keeping the craft paper arrangement hanging on the wall, mark each paper with the spot where the frame's nail should be placed. When the paper is on the wall, hammer it directly into the mark on the paper, then tear the paper away.

4. Hang pictures and enjoy your beautiful gallery wall.

Dry-Erase CALENDAR

JUNE

SU	M	T	W	TH	F	SA
				1	2	3 Bella's Party
4	5 Camp	6	7	8	9	10
11	12	13 Dentist 3:15	14	15	16	17
18	19	20	21	22	23 DAD's Birthday!	24
25 Sarah's Birthday!	26	27	28	29	30	

If you make your calendar into a display-worthy work of art, you'll never miss an assignment again. Use a bold frame and colors that energize you to keep your life on track!

Supplies

pencil

ruler

16 x 20-inch sheet of white poster board

16 x 20-inch picture frame with glass

washi tape (2 colors)

letter stickers

dry-erase marker

Steps

1. Using pencil and ruler, divide poster board into a grid with 6 rows across and 7 columns down. (Do not draw boxes in the top row. It will be open for the month label.) Each box will be about 2 $\frac{7}{8}$ inches wide by 2 $\frac{11}{16}$ inches tall.

2. Place washi tape across grid over pencil lines to divide calendar.

3. Add sticker letters to abbreviate the days of the week over the top stripe of washi tape. Insert poster board in frame.

4. Using dry-erase marker on the glass, write in current month at the top. Number each box for days in the current month, making sure you start the month on the right day of the week.

5. Ask a parent if you can nail on your wall. Keep dry-erase markers nearby to mark important dates!

Clothesline PHOTO DISPLAY

Surround yourself with photos you love and create beautiful paper frames to make them into works of art. Hang them on cute "clotheslines" and swap out as desired to keep your collection current!

Supplies

photos	utility knife
scrapbook paper	tape
ruler	string or ribbon
pencil	mini clothespins
scissors	thumbtacks
thick cardboard	

Steps

1. Choose a photo and scrapbook paper that complements it for the frame. Cut an 8 ½ x 11-inch rectangle from the paper.

2. On the back side of each paper frame, fold in the edges about ½ inch all the way around. Tape them down.

3. Still on the back side, measure and trace a rectangle that is a little smaller than the photo. This is the hole the picture will show through. You can center your cut-out or move it closer to the top of the frame, as shown.

4. Set paper frame still facedown on top of the cardboard to protect work surface. With permission, use utility knife or scissors to cut out the traced rectangle.

5. Tape picture inside. Repeat process for each photo.

6. Hang frames on a string with mini clothespins. Tack string to wall to make a clothesline display!

LOL

SAY
CHEESE!

Washi Tape
FRAMES

Washi tape is a decorator's dream! You can stick it, reposition it, and stick it again, all without damaging surfaces. Use it to make funky frames around magazine clippings, photos, or graphic art for a whimsical look that you can update as often as you like!

Supplies

artwork
double-sided tape
variety of washi tape

Steps

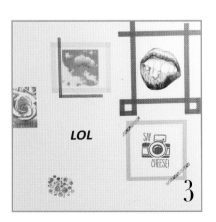

1. Find artwork you want to showcase.

2. Use double-sided tape and arrange pictures on wall. Leave plenty of room around each for frame.

3. Add funky washi tape frames around each piece of art. Mix and match or even overlap frames so they're all unique.

4. Enjoy your gallery!

Glam Decor
& MORE!

Being surrounded by things you love will brighten your day and make you feel your best!

Stenciled
DOOR

Make an entrance! The door to your room is a great spot to show off your style. Be bold! Paint it one bright color, two-tone it, or get creative with stencils to put your room love *on display!*

AFTER

BEFORE

Tip

Dab paint roller or brush on a paper towel before brushing onto stencil to avoid paint drips.

Paint Supplies

medium-grade sandpaper

slightly damp paper towel

drop cloth

painter's tape

1 quart latex paint with primer

paintbrush (1 ½–2 inches wide)

paint roller (4-inch)

paint tray

Stencil Supplies

stencils of your choice

tape measure

painter's tape

acrylic paint

stencil brush

small paintbrush for touch-ups
   (with door paint color)

Painting Steps

1. Sand door.

2. Wipe down with damp paper towel to remove all dirt and residue. Allow to dry.

3. Lay drop cloth under the door to protect work area.

4. Cover anything difficult to paint around with painter's tape, such as doorknob, hinges, and door frame. Carefully apply paint around these areas with brush.

5. If the door is flat, you can use the paint tray and roller to paint the entire door. If the door has panels, use brush instead. Paint in up and down motions. Allow to dry overnight before closing.

Stenciling Steps

1. If you painted the door first, allow 1–2 days for paint to dry before stenciling.

2. Plan stencil design and arrange stencils on door using painter's tape. If you're using the same stencil multiple times, measure where each stencil should go and mark perimeter for each with painter's tape.

3. Use stencil brush to blot on paint over first stencil. Carefully remove tape and stencil. Allow the stencil to dry (or rinse and dry it) before moving it to the next taped spot.

4. Repeat until you have achieved desired design.

5. Use small paintbrush and base door color to touch up any areas with unwanted stencil paint.

Mood
DOOR HANGER

If you're not in the mood to talk about your feelings, you can give others a heads up on your status with a mood symbol! A sunshine, a storm cloud, and everything in between will let the world know whether to give you space, a hug, or a high five!

Supplies

newspapers	yellow cardstock
door hanger	scissors
acrylic paint	black permanent marker
paintbrush	pastel crayons
large drinking glass	washi tape
(or round template	envelope
a bit wider than	self adhesive hook and
door hanger)	loop fasteners
pencil	thumbtack and string

○ ○

Steps

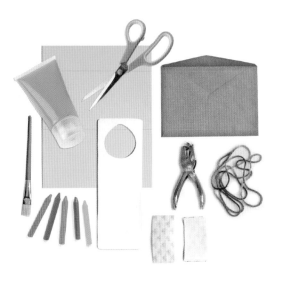

1. Prepare your work area with newspapers. Paint the door hanger.

2. Use the top of the drinking glass to trace circles onto yellow cardstock. (It's more fun if the circles are big enough to hang just over the edge of the door hanger.)

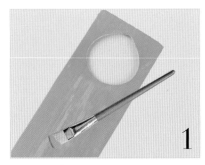

3. Cut out the circles and draw your pictures on them with black marker and pastel crayons. Use weather pictures, faces, or other symbols to express your moods.

4. Once the door hanger is dry, add washi tape trim and write "mood" or "Today is . . ." in black marker. Leave room for a circle below the label.

5. Cut a 1 x 1-inch piece of the "hook" (rough) side of fastener and adhere to the door hanger where the circle will be placed. Adhere a small piece of the "loop" (soft) side of the fastener to the back of each paper circle.

6. Decorate the envelope with washi tape and place the circles inside.

7. Hang your door hanger on the door knob. Tape up or tack the envelope to your door with string. Stick the mood circle to the hanger that reflects your mood today!

Dream
CATCHER

Make a beautiful dream catcher to inspire good dreams! Anything goes in decorating your catcher — ribbons, feathers found on the beach, or beads from old friendship bracelets will make it meaningful and uniquely yours!

Supplies

embroidery hoop

thick yarn

scissors

doily (about size of hoop)

ribbon, lace, leather strips, etc.

beads

feathers

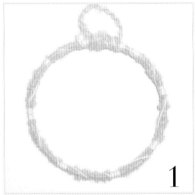

Steps

1. Wrap yarn around your hoop to cover it. Secure with a knot and make a loop at the top for hanging.

2. Cut 12 small pieces of yarn. Loop each piece of yarn through holes at doily's perimeter and tie to hoop. Spread ties evenly around the circle. Use double knots and cut off excess when done.

3. Cut varying lengths of ribbon, lace, leather, and stringed beads. Tie a feather to the end of some pieces.

4. Tie all onto the bottom of the hoop.

5. Hang on your headboard or ask a parent if you can nail above your bed. Happy dreams!

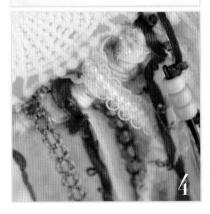

Fairy LIGHTS

Fairy lights can add a cozy, magical feel to any space. Use these pretty light strings to frame a focal point in your room, write an inspiring word, or drape around objects like a mirror, shelves, or desk.

Supplies

LED fairy lights
thumbtacks or tape

Steps

1. Determine what design you'd like to make with the lights.

2. Tack or tape the end of the fairy lights and begin draping the lights. Use tape to secure into the position you desire.

3. Turn on the fairy lights and enjoy the new energy they bring to your room!

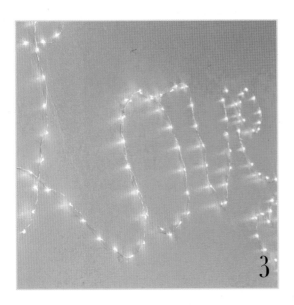

Safety First

LED fairy lights are the safest choice because they are always cool to the touch.

Fabulous
LAMP

Have an outdated, uninspired light fixture? Might be time for a lamp revamp! You can give both the shade and the base a makeover that will shed new light on your style.

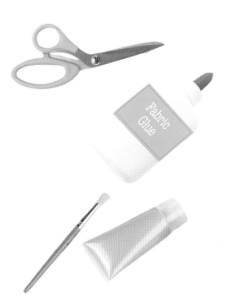

Supplies

lamp with shade

newspapers

acrylic paint

paintbrush

wide, embellished trim piece
   or ribbon from fabric store
   (length needed will depend
   on size of lampshade)

fabric glue

scissors

○ ○

Steps

1. Remove lampshade and set aside. Spread out newspapers to protect work surface.

2. Paint lamp base a color that complements your lampshade trim. Allow to dry.

3. Beginning at the top of the lampshade, apply a line of fabric glue around the top perimeter of the shade. Press on the fabric trim a little at a time, working your way around the shade. Continue applying more glue and more fabric, wrapping the lampshade with trim.

4. When you reach the bottom of the lamp, cut off the end of the trim and apply a bit more glue to stick the tail to the lamp.

5. Reassemble your lamp and light up your space!

Room SCENTS

Whether you want to chill out or charge up, different aromas can put you in the right frame of mind. Try out these DIY scent jars to lift your spirits and infuse your space with fabulous fragrance!

GINGER ORANGE
1 orange sliced in rings
2 cinnamon sticks
½ tbsp cloves
3 slices fresh ginger
1 tsp almond extract

Supplies

kitchen utensils

ingredients noted for each scent

canning jars with ring tops

paper cupcake liners

twine or raffia ribbon

embellishments for lid such as buttons or plastic jewels

bamboo skewer

Steps

1

1. Use the recipes shown to combine ingredients in each jar.

2. Top off jar with water (except for coffee bean recipe).

3. Place cupcake paper on top of jar.

4. Place the ring on top of cupcake paper and screw on. Tie a piece of twine or ribbon around it. Add embellishment if desired.

5. Poke holes in cupcake paper using skewer

6. Leave jar in your room up to 2 weeks and enjoy the aroma!

4

COFFEE BEAN
orange and cinnamon essential oils
enough coffee beans to fill jar (no water)
1 tsp baking soda

HERB LEMON
2 lemons sliced in rings
6 sprigs fresh rosemary
1 tsp vanilla extract

MINTY LIME
3 limes sliced in rings
6 sprigs fresh thyme
8 fresh mint leaves

5

Disco BALL

Bring some bling and sparkle to your space with a DIY disco ball! Quick and easy to make, this retro decor will add free-spirited fun to your room.

Supplies

paper lantern
string
tape measure
silver party paper
scissors
rubber cement or clear adhesive

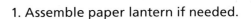

Steps

1

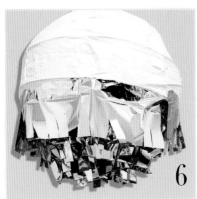

6

1. Assemble paper lantern if needed.

2. While crafting, hang lantern securely in a position that is easy for you to work with.

3. With a piece of string, measure the circumference of the lantern. Place string on a tape measure to determine the length and add 6 inches extra for overlap.

4. Cut 10 strips of silver paper the length of your measurement. Each strip should be about 5 inches wide.

5. Along the length of each strip, cut a fringe every 1–2 inches, cutting about halfway up the strip width.

6. Spread rubber cement on the bottom parts of the lantern and wrap the first silver strip around it. Continue layering glue and silver paper until the disco ball is completely covered. (There will be a lot of overlap toward the top and bottom of lantern as the distance around is smaller there.) Hang the ball in your room and turn up the music!

Tip

Use a hot glue gun to wrap a plain vase with yarn to coordinate with your pom-poms!

Pom-Pom FLOWERS

Bring spring to your room with these gorgeous faux flowers. Using real twigs is a great way for nature lovers to bring the outdoors in!

Supplies

scissors
ruler
yarn in various colors
fork
hot glue gun and glue
twigs
vase

Steps

1. Cut a 6-inch piece of yarn and thread it through middle tine of the fork. Hold tail ends in place with your fingers.

2. Begin wrapping more yarn around all the fork tines, holding down the original tails. The more you wrap, the thicker the pom pom will be. Leave a small tail.

3. When finished, release the 6-inch yarn and pull both ends up to the top of the fork tines, over the wrapped yarn. Tie it once around the wrapped yarn on the fork.

4. Slide yarn off the fork. Tug tightly and tie 6-inch yarn in a double knot. Now cut through the wrapped loops.

5. Fluff out the pom and trim as needed.

6. Glue finished poms to the twigs and arrange in a vase.

Photo
BOOTH

Create an old-school photo booth in your room with silly props and a glam backdrop for impromptu selfie sessions. Ask your friends to help you make extra props to keep your selfies funny, fresh, and fabulous!

Supplies

props for photos (hats, scarves, masks, funny glasses, etc.)
basket or bin to hold props
backdrop (pretty sheet, banners, paper chains, tapestry, LED lights, etc.)
tape or thumbtacks
phone camera

Steps

1. Find a space in your room for a photo booth. A corner without any backlight works best.

2. Gather props for photo booth. Collect them in a basket and keep near the booth.

3. Decide on a theme and collect materials for backdrop.

4. Look around the house or visit thrift or craft stores to find additional fun props or different backdrops for variety.

5. Hang backdrop with tape or thumbtacks and get started on your selfie sessions!

Dream JAR

Think of big and small dreams or words of inspiration — things that will bring you joy or make your life spectacular. Anything from "I want to have five dogs," to "Be creative in every way you can!" Whenever you need a pick-me-up, grab one and be inspired.

Supplies

pretty paper
scissors
ruler
pencil or pen
glass jar with lid
twine or string
gift tag or label tag
hole punch

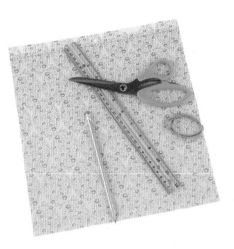

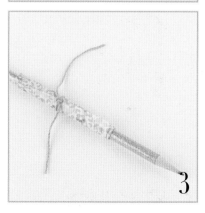

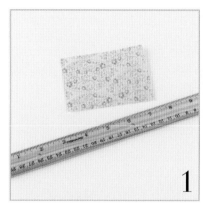

Steps

1. Cut pieces of paper into 3 x 4-inch rectangles.

2. Write a dream or message on the plain back side of each paper.

3. Roll up paper around a pencil to make a scroll. Tie scroll with twine.

4. Pull out pencil and put scroll in jar.

5. Decorate jar with ribbons or beads.

6. Make a label for the jar. Use a hole punch if needed and tie it on with string.

Room Love and Craft It Yourself are published by
Capstone Young Readers
A Capstone Imprint
1710 Roe Crest Drive
North Mankato, Minnesota 56003
www.mycapstone.com

Library of Congress Cataloging-in-Publication Data is available on the
Library of Congress website.

ISBN: 978-1-62370-817-7

Summary: A craft and project book to help redecorate, organize,
and make a bedroom space reflect personal style.

Editor: Kristen Mohn
Designer: Lori Bye
Creative Director: Heather Kindseth

Projects crafted by:
Heather Wutschke, Lori Bye, Shelli Frana, Amy Trina,
Karon Dubke, Marcy Morin, and Sarah Schuette

Image credits:
All photographs by Capstone Studio/Karon Dubke, Heather Kindseth except:
Shutterstock: Analgin, design element, background 112, Angie Makes, quotes 71, Anna Kutukova, words 6, Artnis, design element throughout,
bogdan ionescu, top 105, ConstantinosZ, purple sneakers 65, Curly Pat, (floral) design element throughout, Danilaleo, middle 105, Daria
Minaeva, bottom left 98, Everything, dresser 6, GeniusKp, pink room 6, Glowonconcept, 9, goir, bucket 47, Heiko Kueverling, shoe boxes 64-65,
Iliveinoctober, clouds 6, indigolotos, shoe box 51, shoe boxes 65, IndiPixi, design element, IreneArt, (geometric pattern) design element throughout,
matin, paper 6, Photographee.eu, bedroom 6

Printed and bound in China.
010310F17

About the Author

Heather Wutschke's passion is making her world beautiful — whether that's
by designing children's books, painting with her daughter, or completing DIY
projects to prettify her house. She believes that good design can improve
moods and solve problems. Heather has a degree in graphic design and has
spent her career in advertising and publishing. She lives in Missoula, Montana,
with her husband and their daughter, Raini. When she isn't staying up late
working, she's outside, surrounded by fresh air, mountains, and Montana's
big sky.